MW01620816

Here is a selection of jobs that make our country work. Each one requires special skills, training and lots of practice. Do you know anybody who does one of these jobs? Which jobs would you like to do? Which job is your favorite?

Designer: Jo Rigg
Editor: Rebecca Clunes

We couldn't have made this book without: Jo Douglass, Robert Tainsh, Louisa Beaumont, Claire Cartwright, Sally Poulson and Amy Oliver. We hope you enjoy this book as much as we enjoyed making it.

Originally created by priddy books.

 Published by Scholastic Inc., 557 Broadway, New York, NY 10012, by arrangement with St. Martin's Press.
Printed in the U.S.A.

ISBN 0-439-84631-5

9 10 08 13 12 11 10 09

ABC
OF
JOBS PEOPLE DO

Roger Priddy
with photography by
Richard Brown

SCHOLASTIC INC.
New York Toronto London Auckland Sydney
Mexico City New Delhi Hong Kong Buenos Aires

I fly the planes that take you all over the world. I steer the plane and control how high and how fast it goes. Every day I make sure my passengers get to where they need to go quickly and safely.

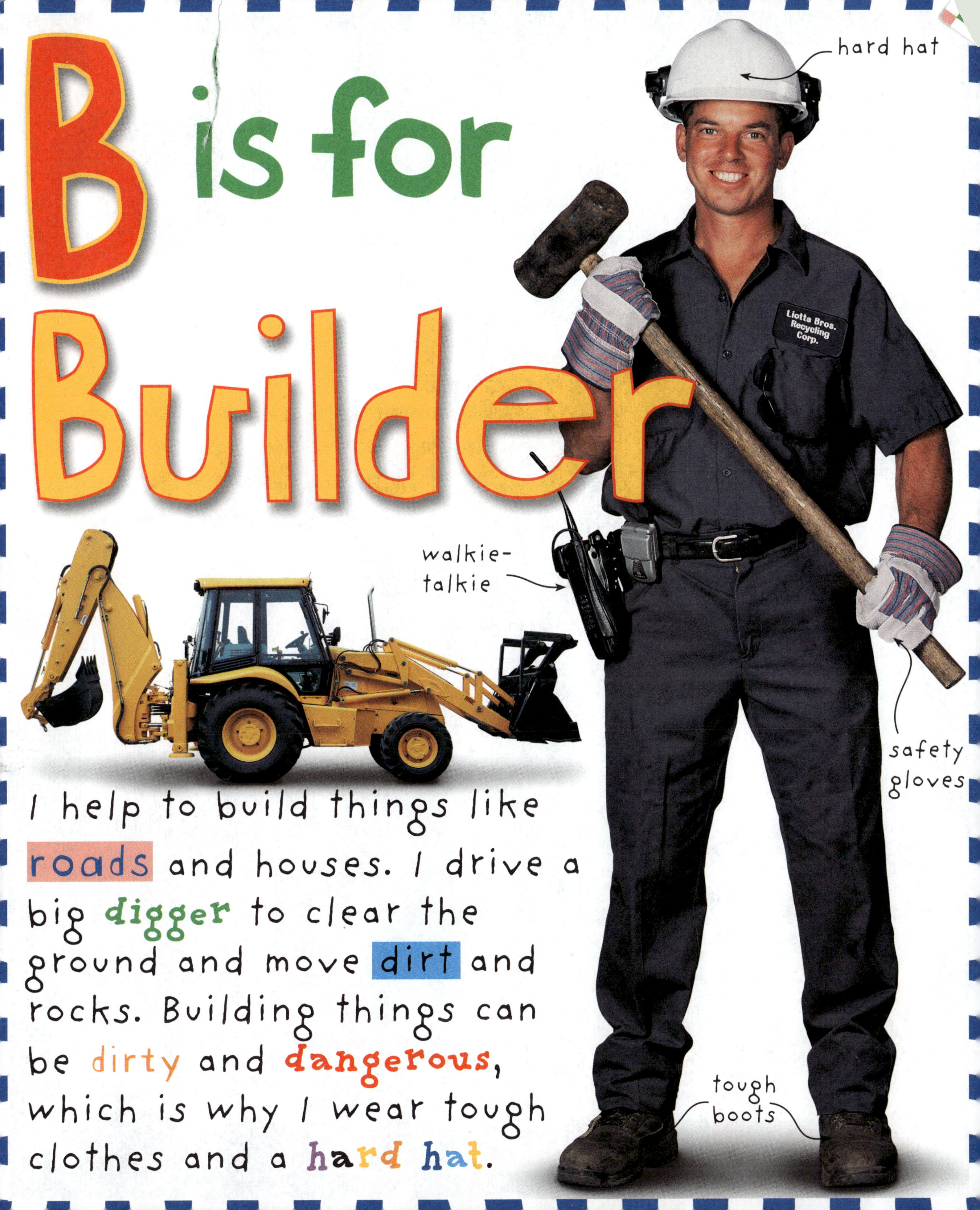

B is for Builder

I help to build things like roads and houses. I drive a big digger to clear the ground and move dirt and rocks. Building things can be dirty and dangerous, which is why I wear tough clothes and a hard hat.

C is for

Lots of people eat in my **restaurant** every day and I work in the kitchen to **prepare** and cook **delicious** meals for my customers. I wear a special **uniform** and keep my kitchen very clean.

Chef

D is for

It's my job to help you keep your teeth and gums healthy so that you always have a nice smile. I take x-rays of your teeth to make sure you don't have cavities and fix them if you do!

Dentist

cell phone

company file

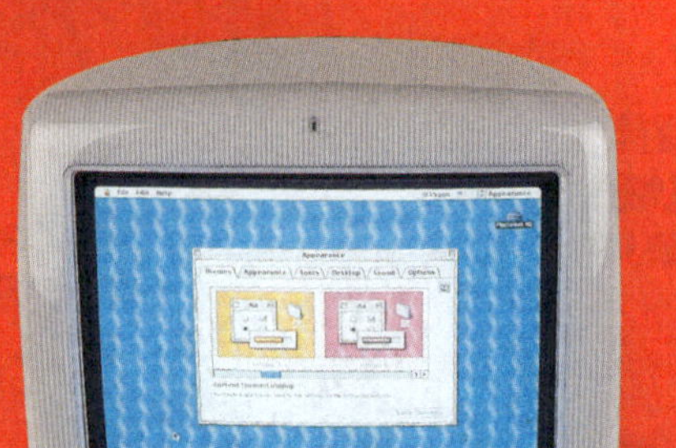

I work in the city and run a **BIG** company. I make decisions and help the people who work for me make the company successful. I am always meeting people so I have to dress professionally.

business clothes

Executive

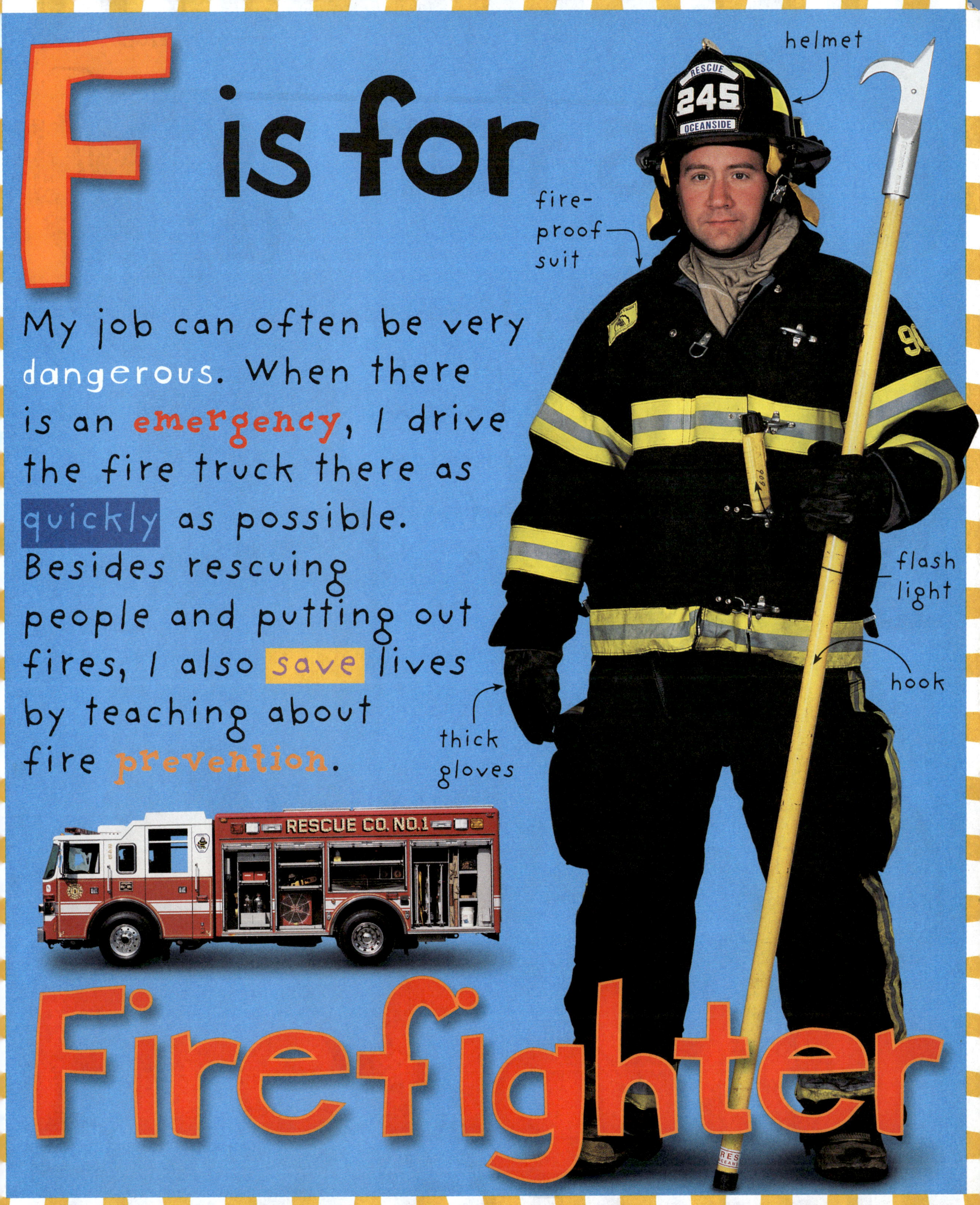
F is for
My job can often be very dangerous. When there is an emergency, I drive the fire truck there as quickly as possible. Besides rescuing people and putting out fires, I also save lives by teaching about fire prevention.
helmet
fire-proof suit
flash light
hook
thick gloves
RESCUE
245
OCEANSIDE
RESCUE CO. NO.1
Firefighter

G is for

I work at a golf course and teach people how to play golf. I show them how to choose the correct golf club and how to hit the ball in the right direction. I also teach them the rules of the game.

Golf Pro

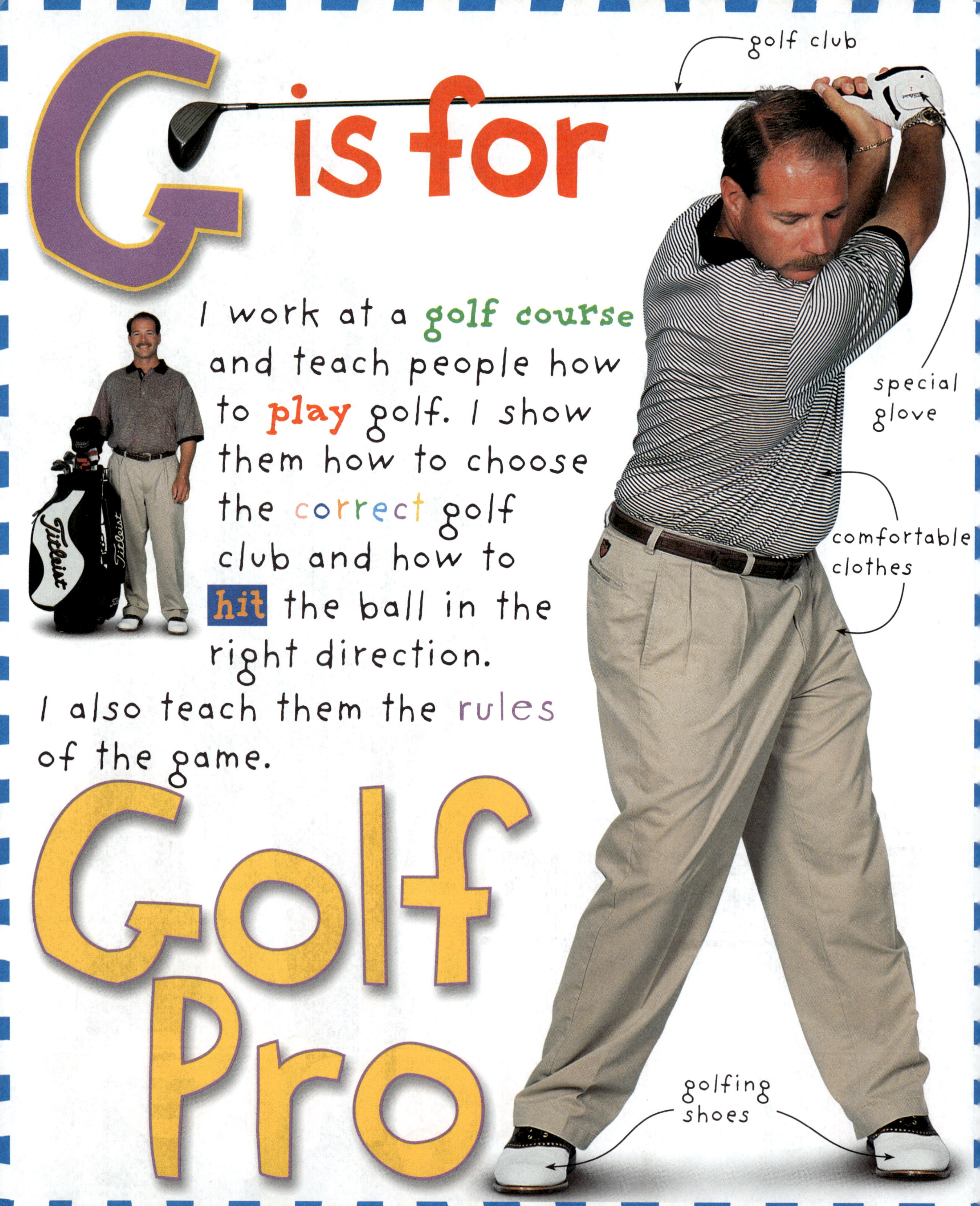

H is for

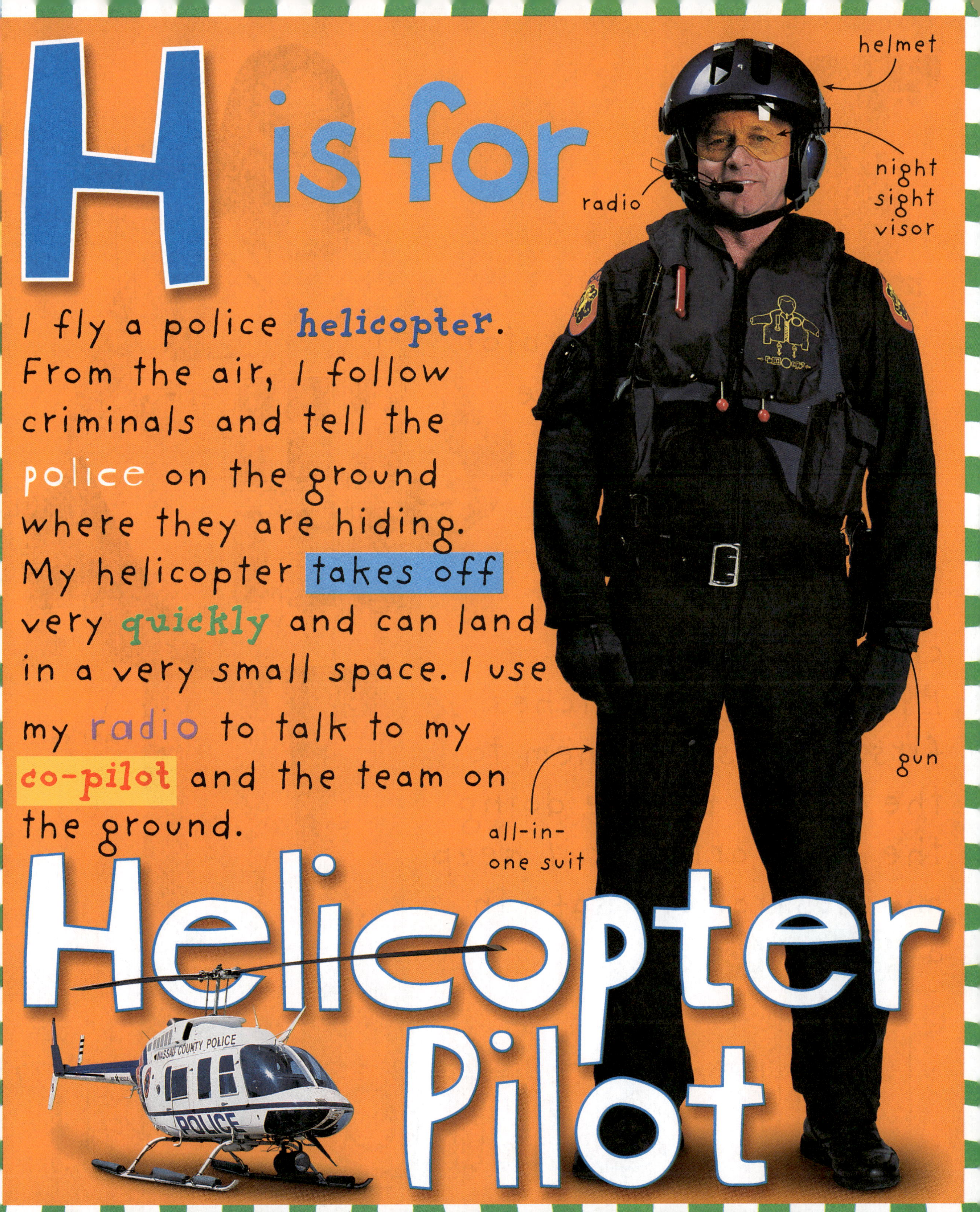

I fly a police **helicopter**. From the air, I follow criminals and tell the police on the ground where they are hiding. My helicopter takes off very **quickly** and can land in a very small space. I use my radio to talk to my **co-pilot** and the team on the ground.

Helicopter Pilot

I is for

An illustrator has to be very good at drawing – I draw pictures for children's books. I make rough sketches first, and show them to the author before doing the final artwork. I keep my illustrations safe in a portfolio.

Illustrator

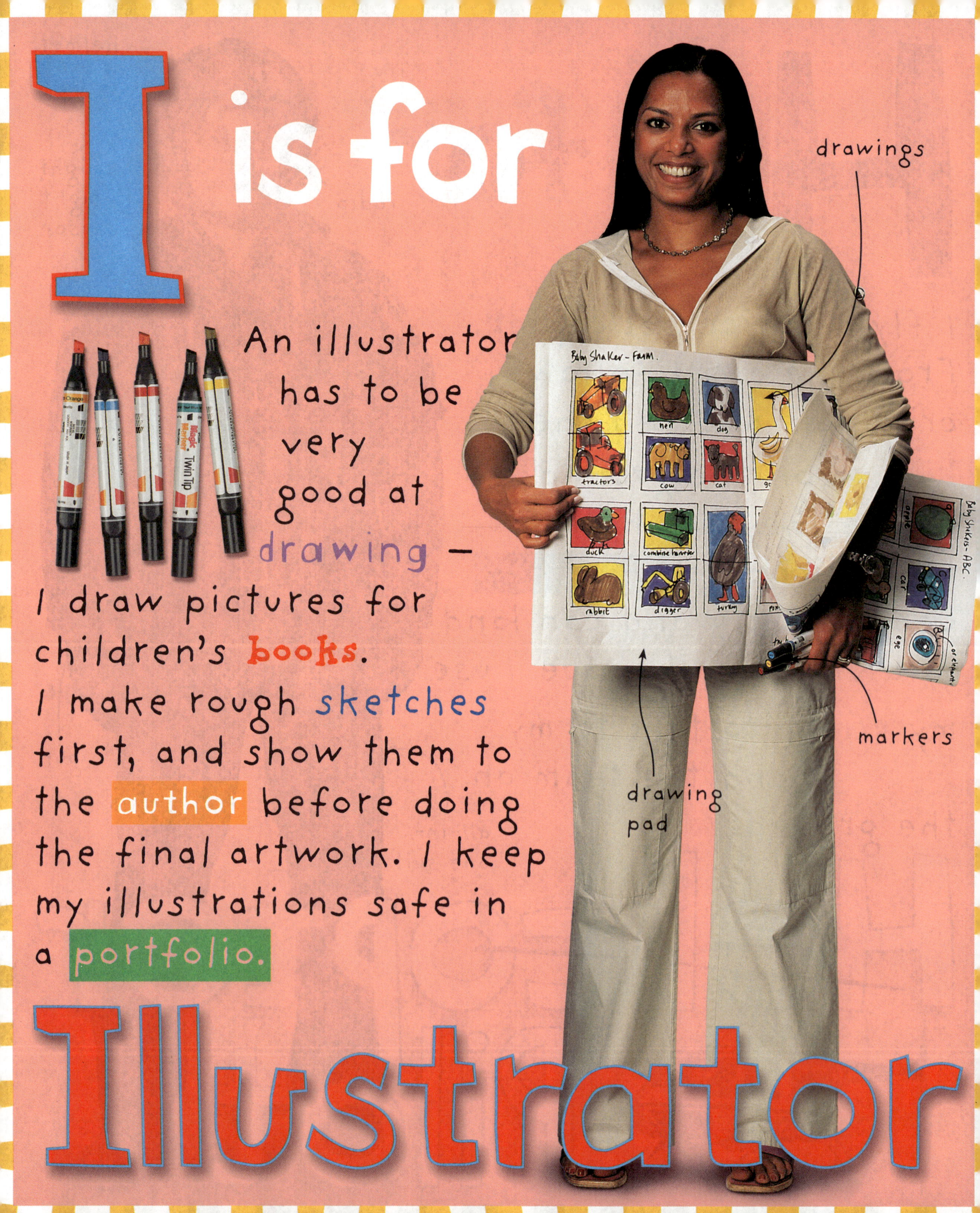

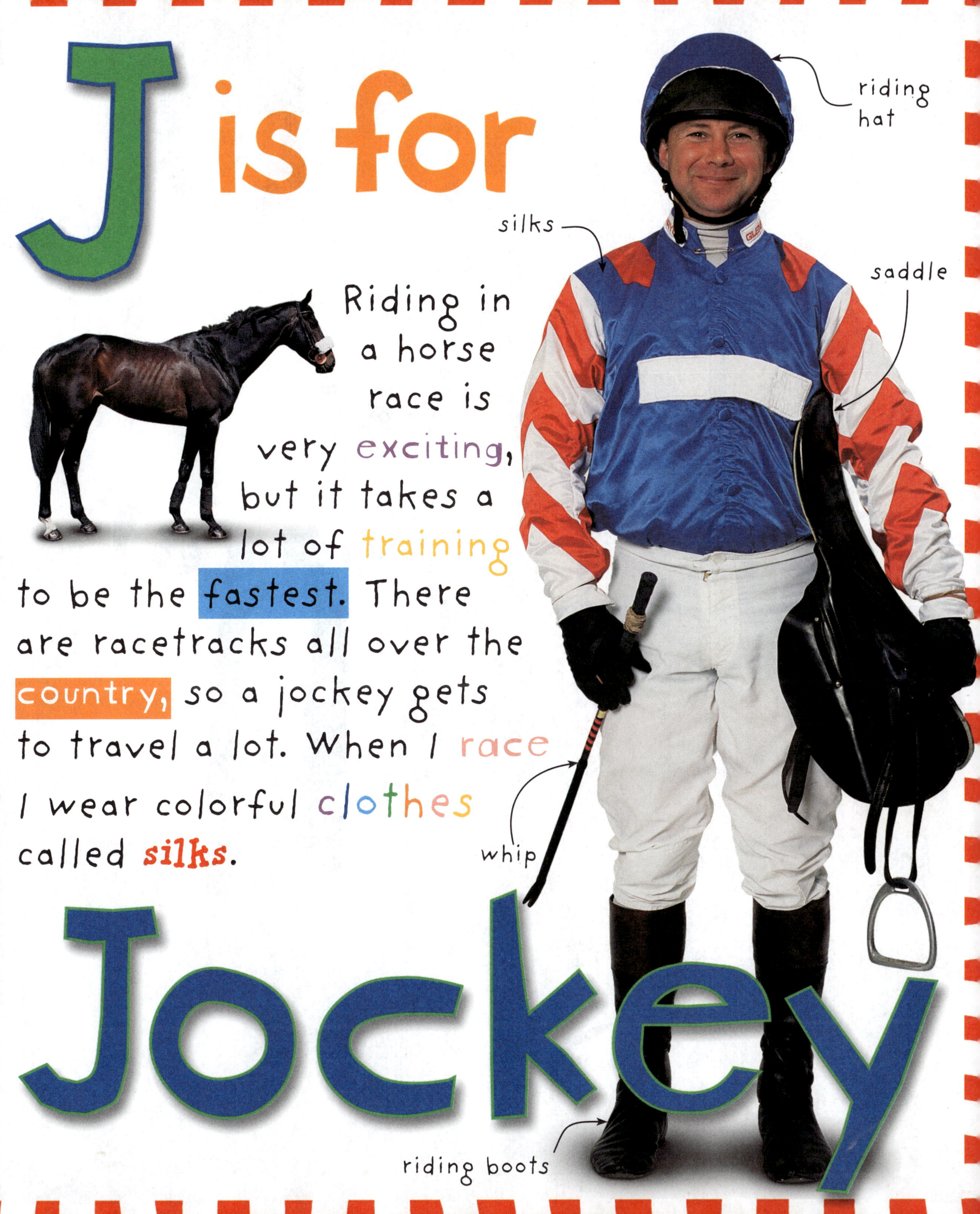
J is for
Riding in a horse race is very exciting, but it takes a lot of training to be the fastest. There are racetracks all over the country, so a jockey gets to travel a lot. When I race I wear colorful clothes called silks.
riding hat
silks
saddle
whip
riding boots
Jockey

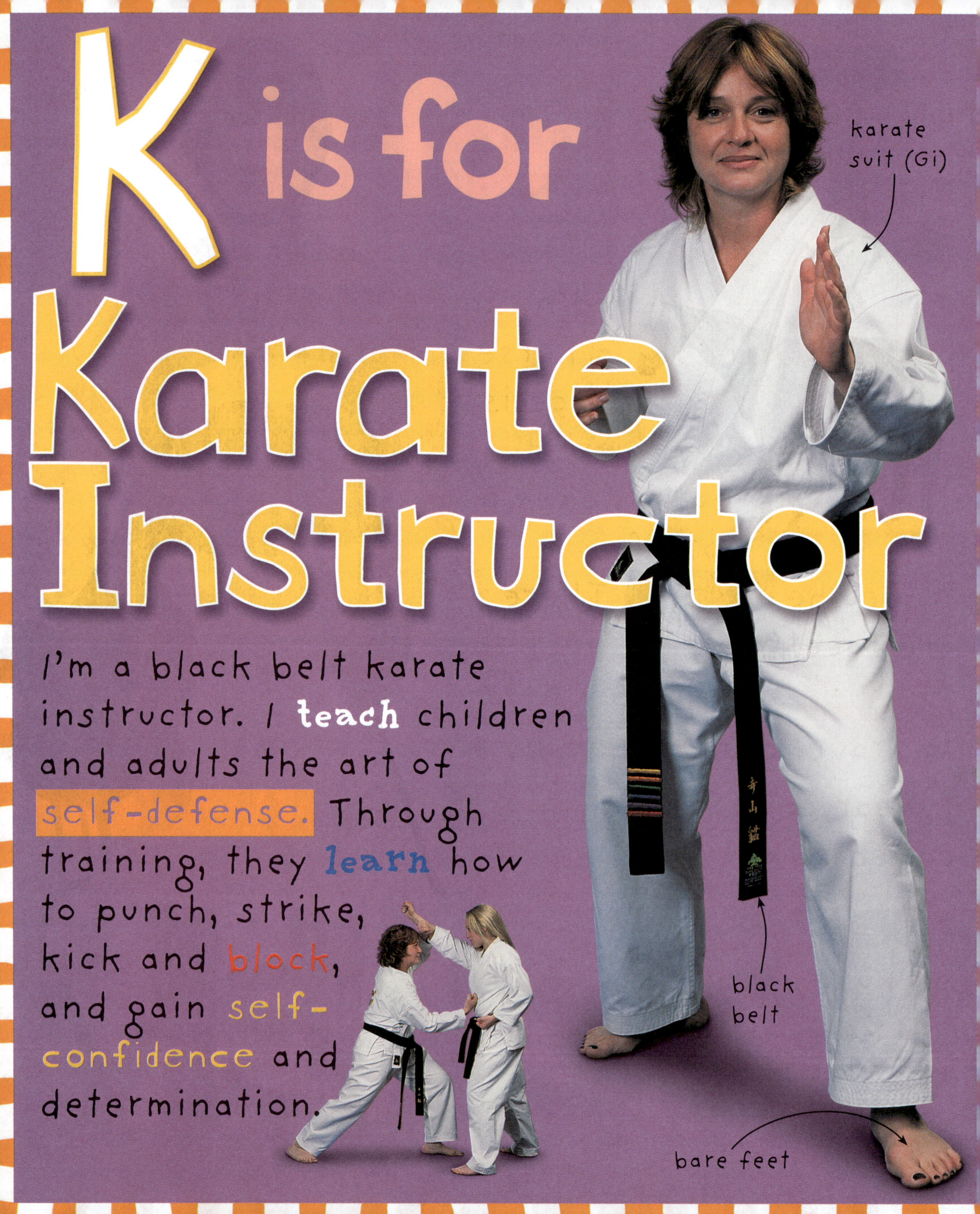

K is for Karate Instructor

I'm a black belt karate instructor. I **teach** children and adults the art of self-defense. Through training, they **learn** how to punch, strike, kick and block, and gain self-confidence and determination.

L is for
It's my job to make people's gardens and yards look beautiful. I cut lawns, trim hedges and plant many colorful flowers and bushes.
Landscape Gardener
cap
thick gloves
garden knife
spade
heavy boots

M is for

I work in a garage where I keep cars running smoothly and safely. I repair them when they break down so I have to know how everything works. I also check the oil, change tires and give tune-ups.

Mechanic

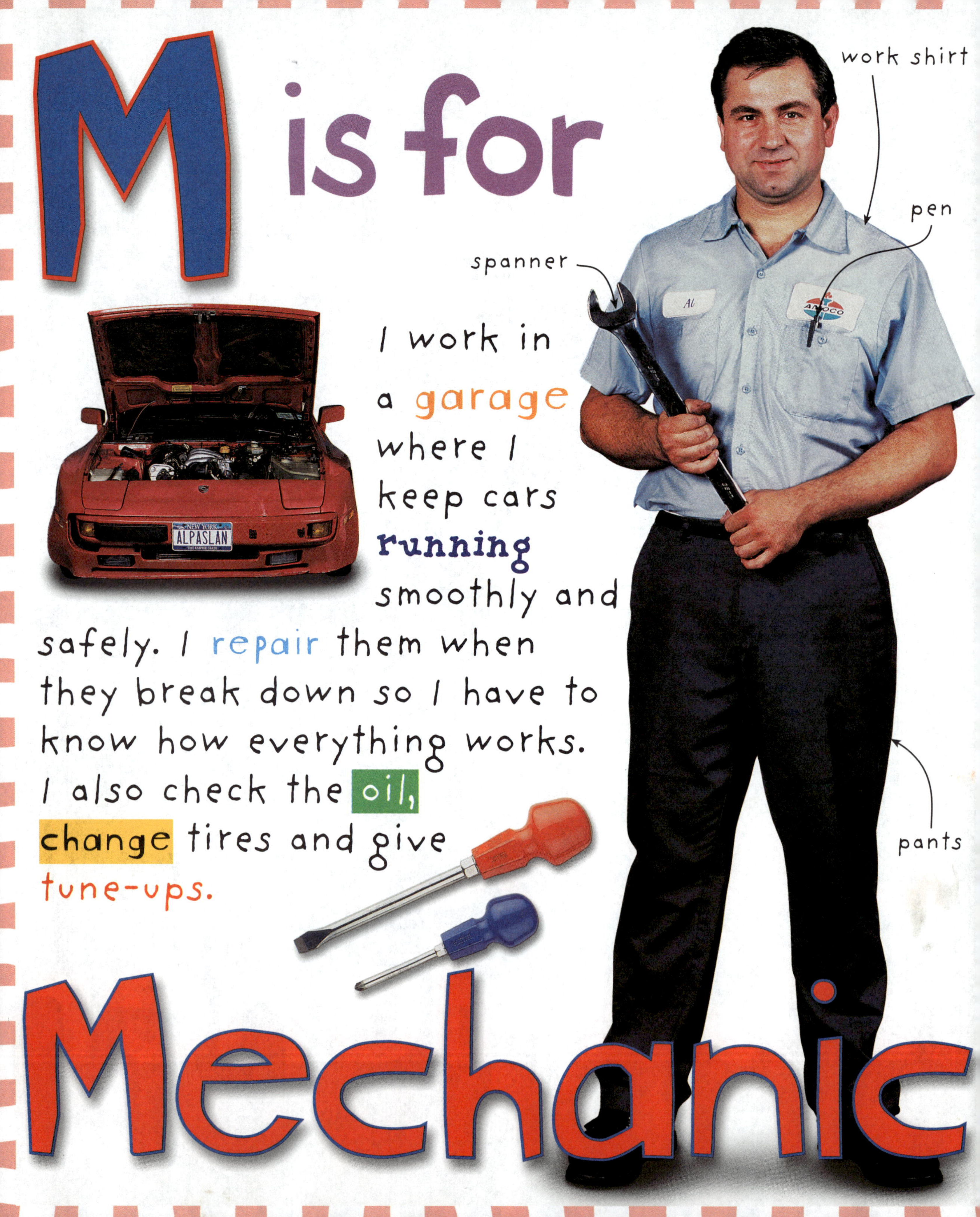

N is for Nurse

If you have to go to the hospital, a nurse like me will take good care of you. I work with doctors to make sick people better. I give out medicine, take temperatures, and bandage wounds.

O is for Obstetrician

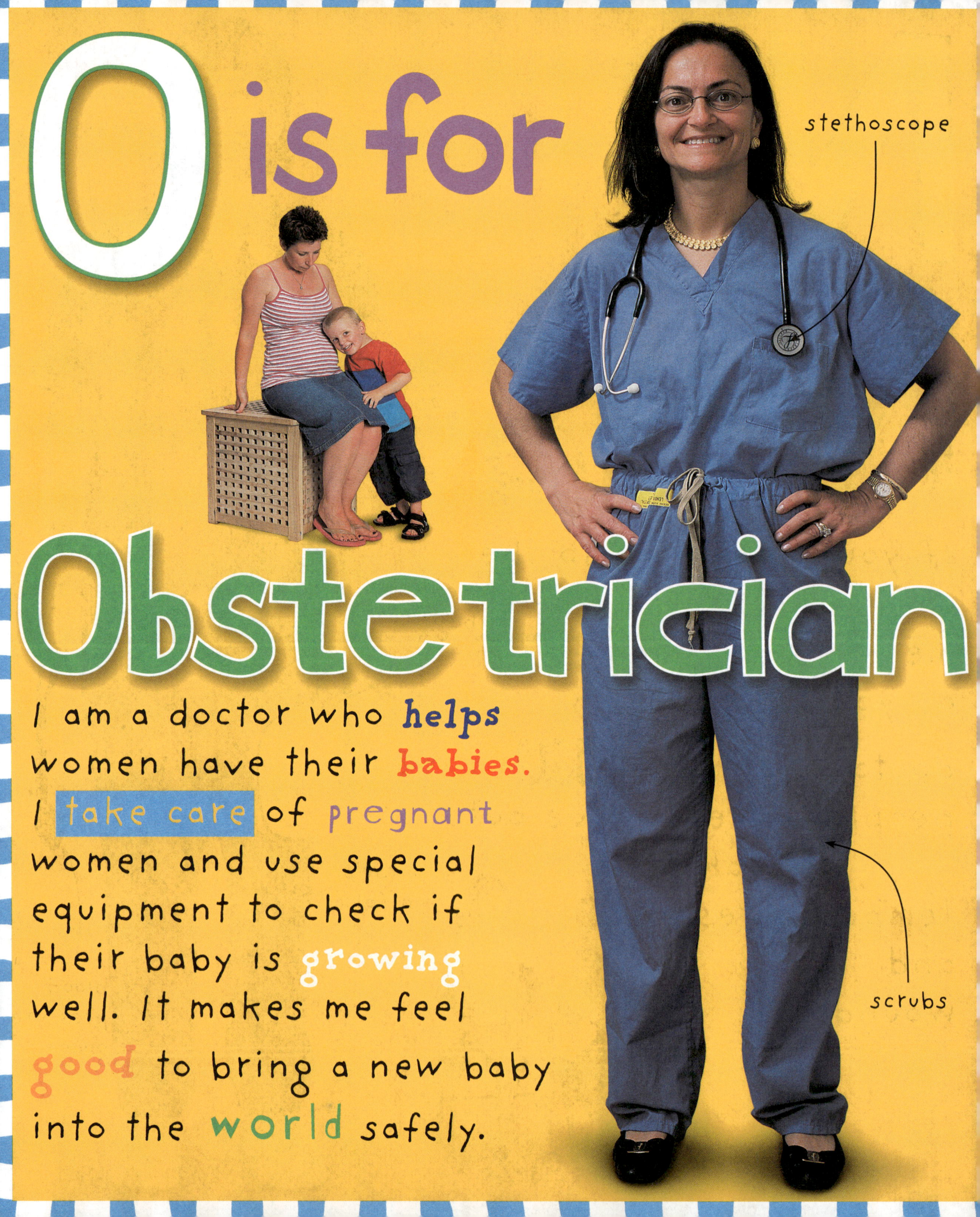

I am a doctor who **helps** women have their **babies.** I take care of pregnant women and use special equipment to check if their baby is growing well. It makes me feel good to bring a new baby into the world safely.

P is for Police Officer

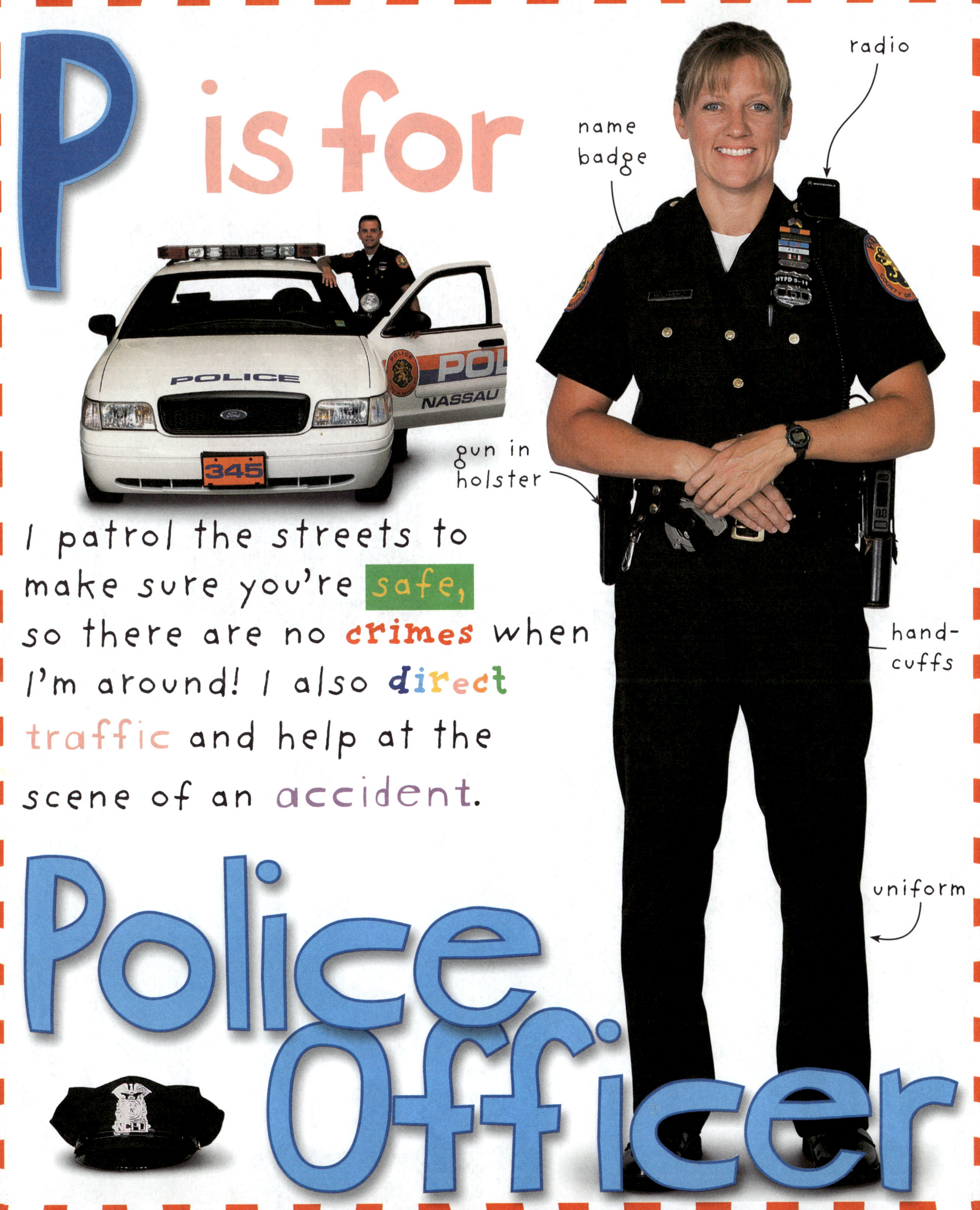

I patrol the streets to make sure you're safe, so there are no crimes when I'm around! I also direct traffic and help at the scene of an accident.

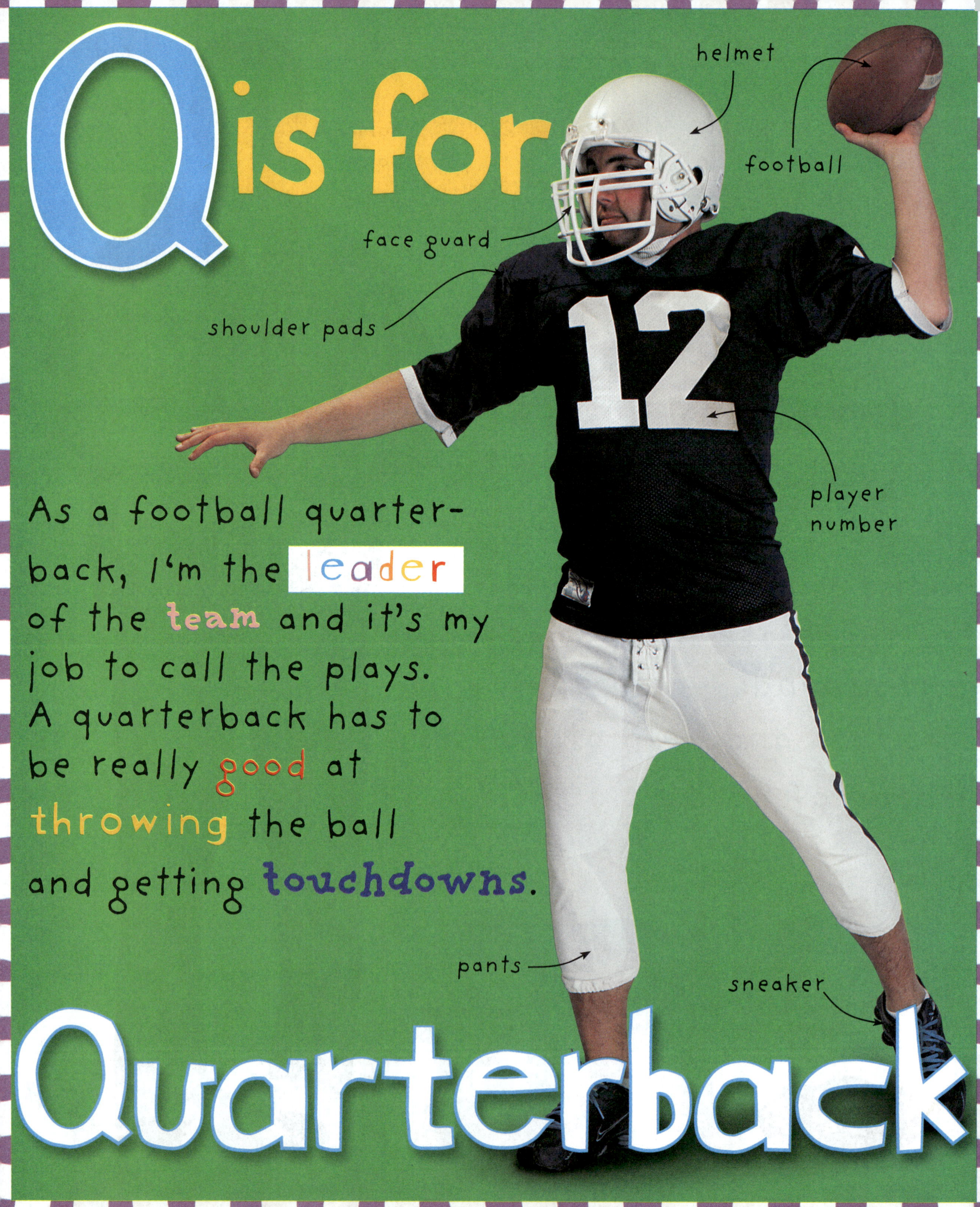
Q is for
helmet
football
face guard
shoulder pads
12
player number
As a football quarter-back, I'm the leader of the team and it's my job to call the plays. A quarterback has to be really good at throwing the ball and getting touchdowns.
pants
sneaker
Quarterback

R is for

Racing a car can be dangerous, but it's also very exciting. I have to concentrate very hard if I want to win. When I'm not racing, I do tests on my car to make sure it goes as fast as it can.

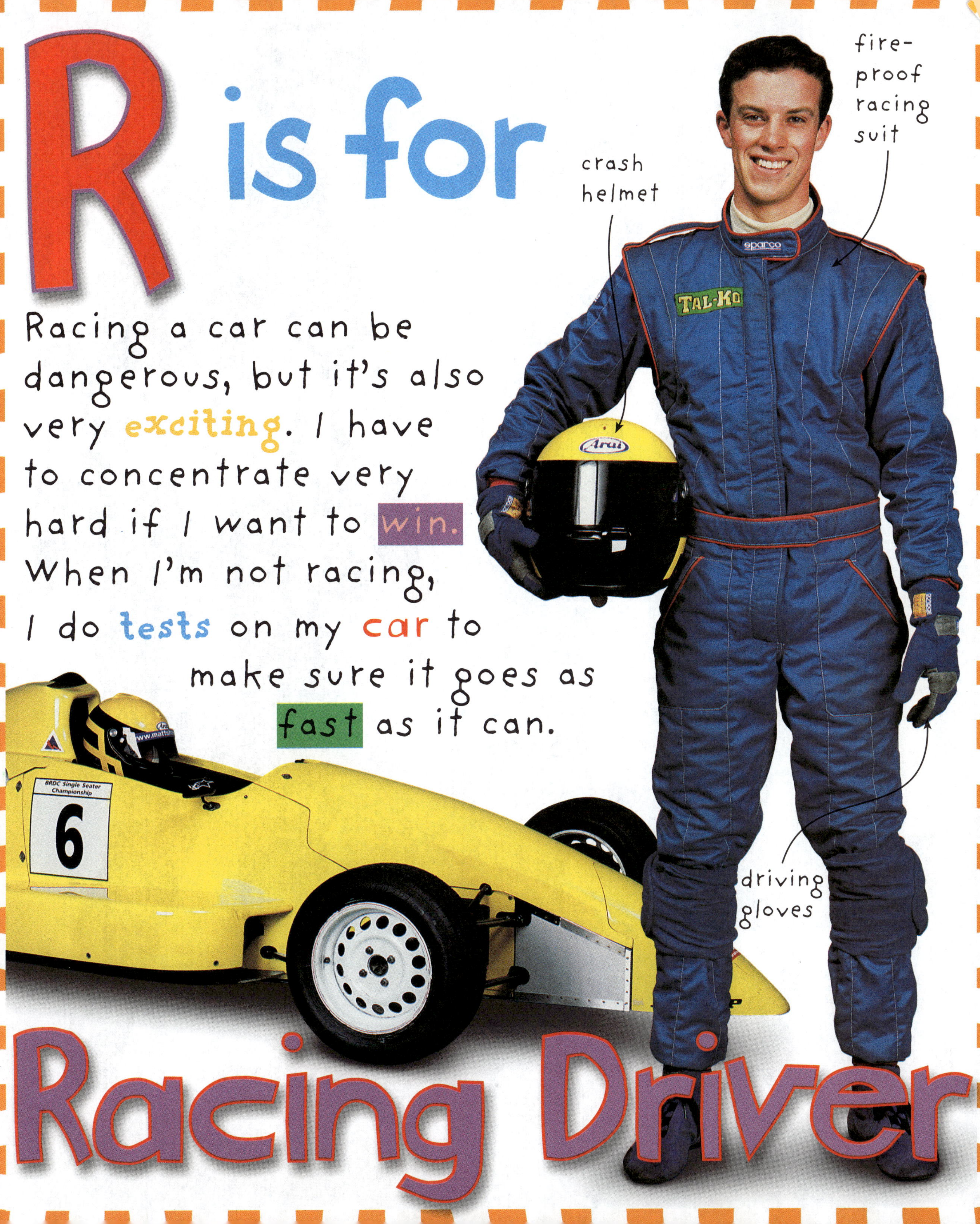

Racing Driver

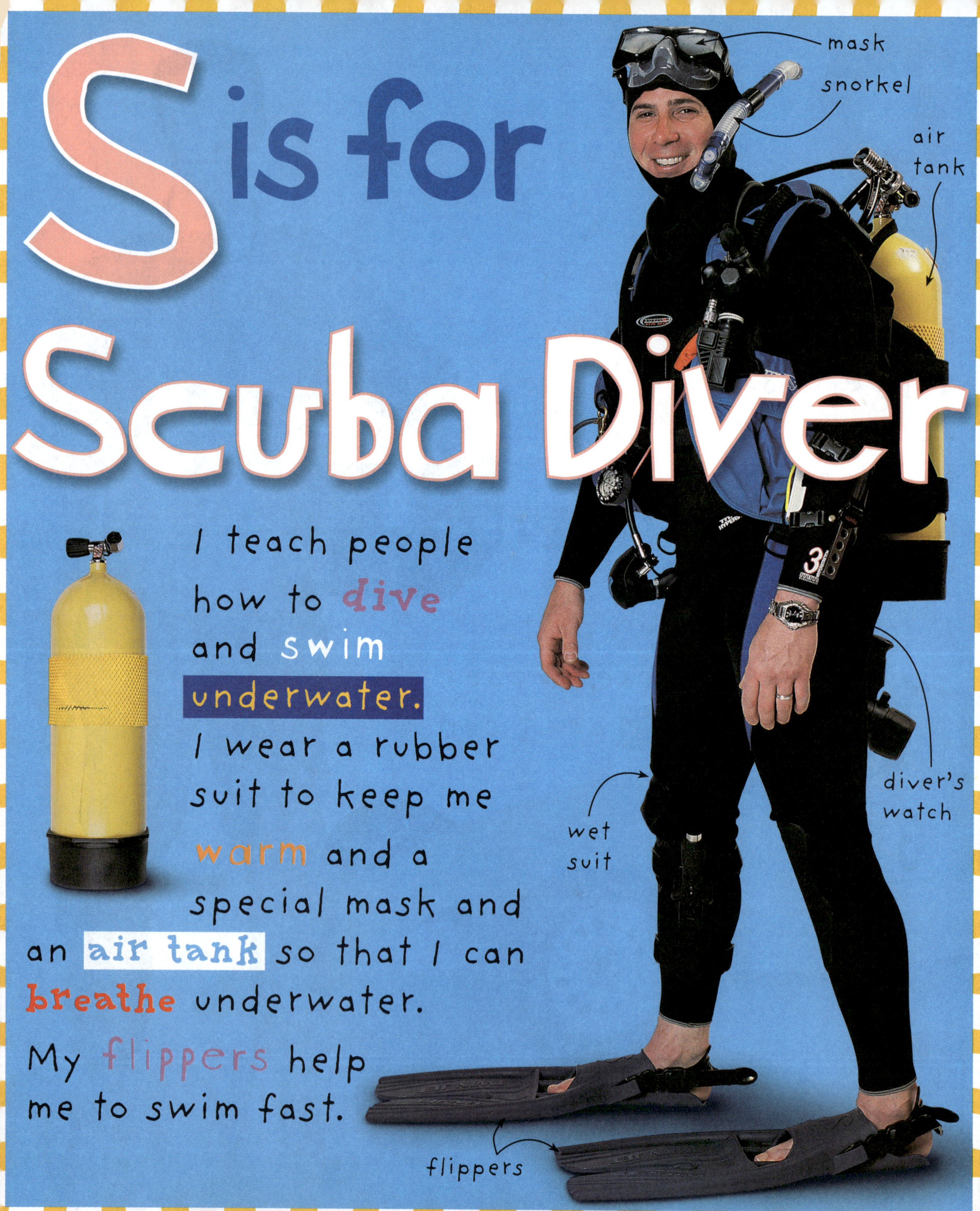

S is for Scuba Diver

I teach people how to dive and swim underwater. I wear a rubber suit to keep me warm and a special mask and an air tank so that I can breathe underwater. My flippers help me to swim fast.

T is for Teacher

I teach students in an elementary school. Some are good at reading, spelling or math and others are better at art, singing or sports. I encourage them to try their best at everything!

U is for

I use my fast boat to respond to emergencies on the water, often when the sea is rough and dangerous. I help people who are lost, give first aid if there's an accident and teach people about water safety.

U.S. Coastguard

V is for

If you love animals and you like hard work, then this is the job for you!

I treat sick pets and help them get better. People have all kinds of pets so I work with snakes and lizards as well as cats and dogs.

Vet

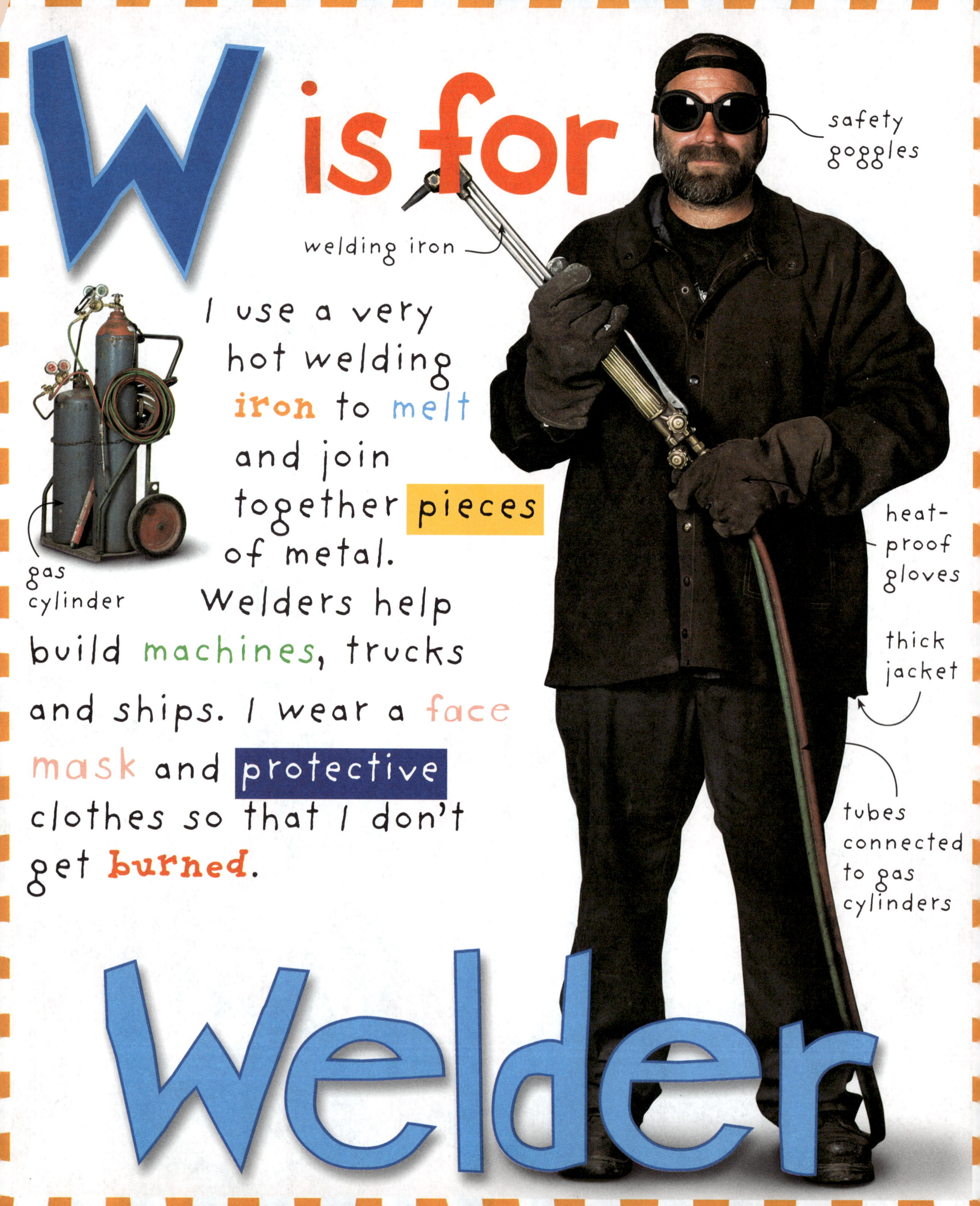
W is for
welding iron
safety goggles
I use a very hot welding iron to melt and join together pieces of metal.
gas cylinder
Welders help build machines, trucks and ships. I wear a face mask and protective clothes so that I don't get burned.
heat-proof gloves
thick jacket
tubes connected to gas cylinders
Welder

X is for
I play in a big orchestra in the percussion section. I strike the wooden bars with my mallets and notes come out of the pipes.
mallets
wooden bars
pipes
Xylophonist

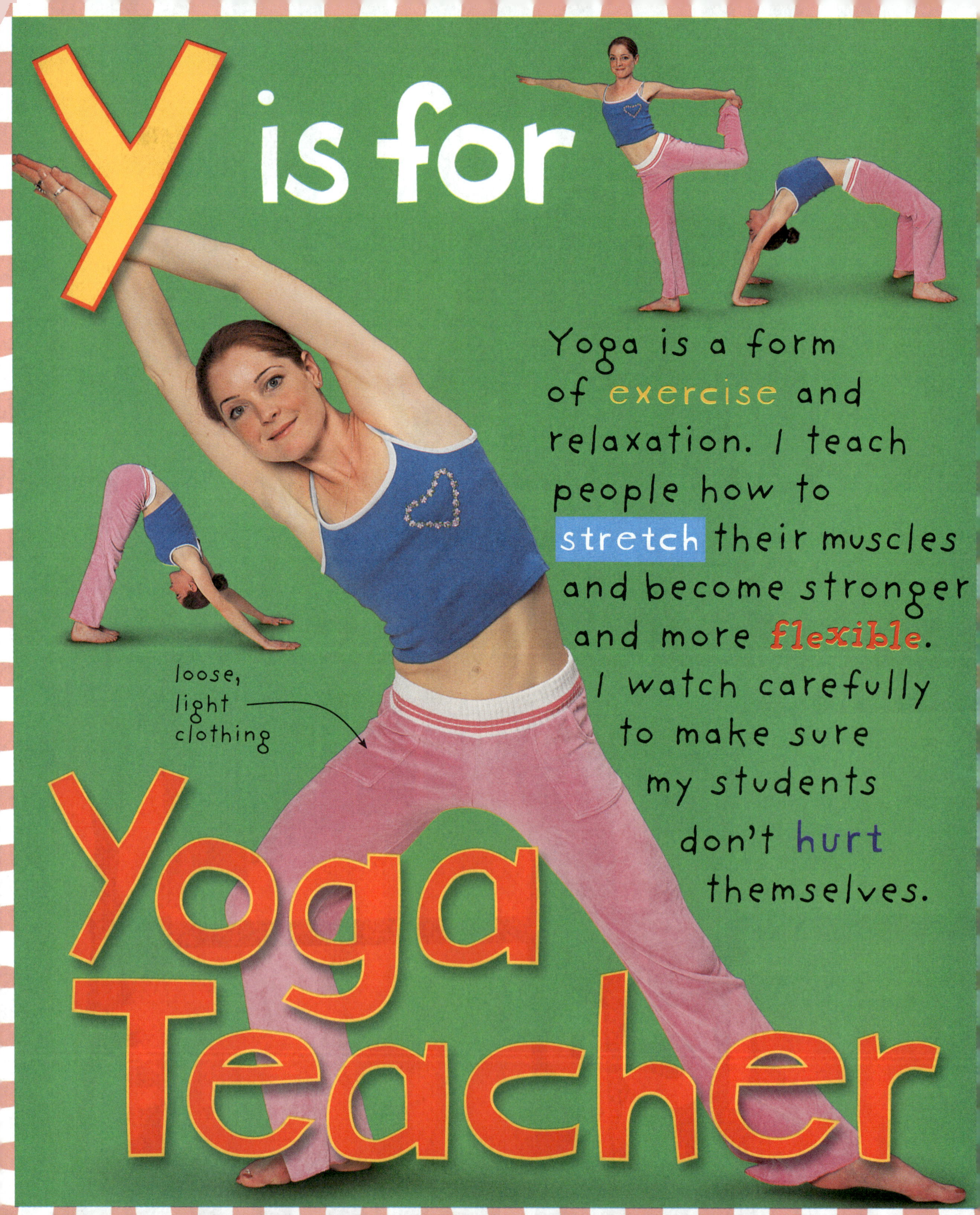
Y is for
Yoga is a form of exercise and relaxation. I teach people how to stretch their muscles and become stronger and more flexible. I watch carefully to make sure my students don't hurt themselves.
loose, light clothing
Yoga Teacher

Z is for Zoo Keeper

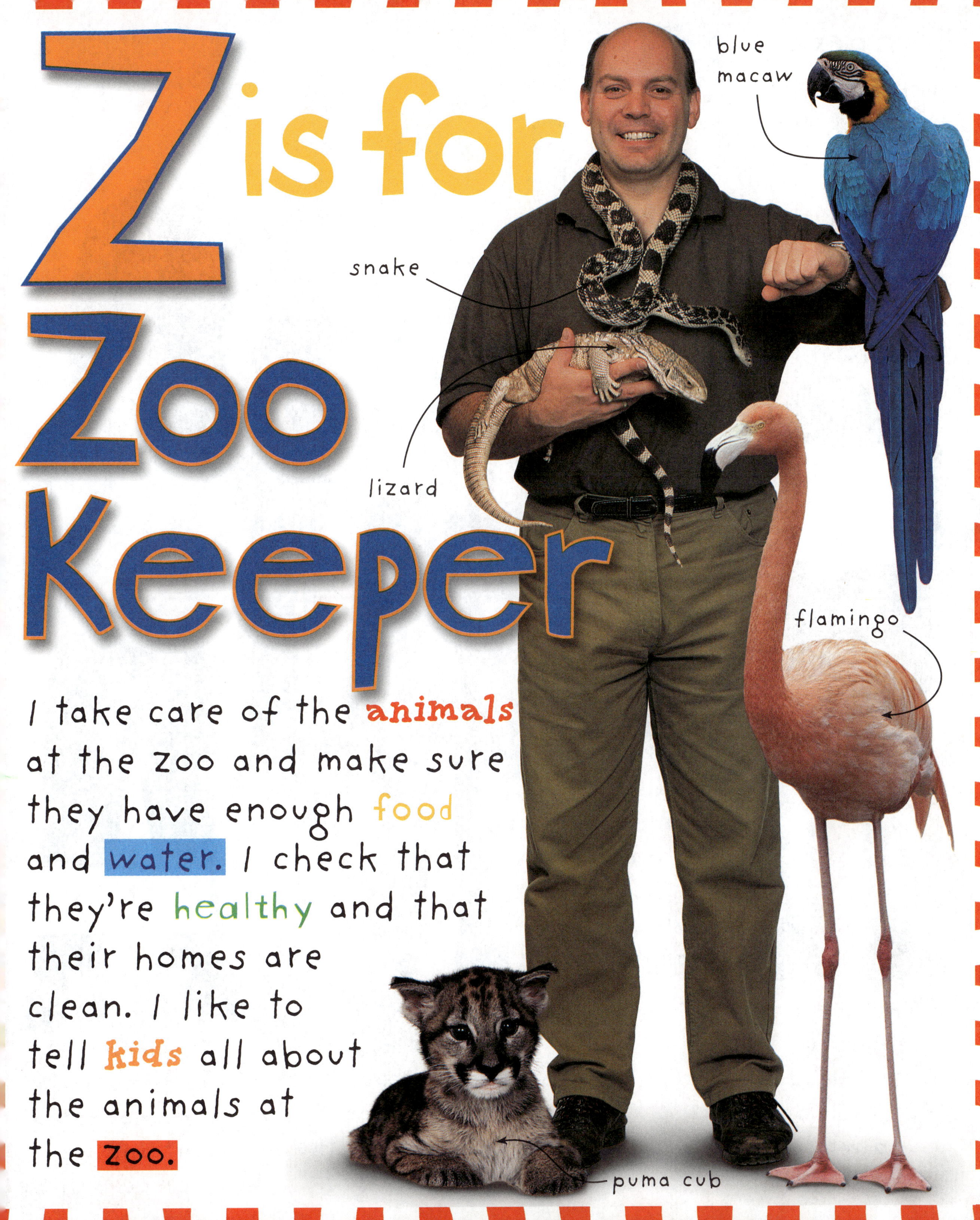

I take care of the **animals** at the zoo and make sure they have enough food and water. I check that they're healthy and that their homes are clean. I like to tell **kids** all about the animals at the zoo.

The people who made this book...
Designer
2
Photographer
The photographer takes the pictures
4
Author
1
3
Editor
The designer decides how the pictures and the words should look on each page
5
Manager
The author comes up with the idea for the book and writes the words
The editor organizes the photo shoots and checks that the words are right
The manager works out how many books to print and what the price will be

6 Production

The production manager decides which printer to use and makes sure the book is delivered on time

7 Printer

The printer works at the factory that prints and makes the book

8 Sales rep

The sales rep visits stores to tell them about the book and persuade them to order lots of copies

9 Store owner

The store owner displays the finished book for you to buy

10 Customer

Reading the book is the best job of all!